This series of handy, instructive volumes shows the reader not only how to draw but how to do so step by step. In this fresh approach the subjects are shown from the earliest sketches to the finished work. The authors are all artists who are expert in their own fields of art. The titles in this series are:

These **Watson-Guptill Studio Drawing Books** are now available to schools and libraries in **GOLDENCRAFT BINDING** from GOLDEN PRESS, INC. Educational Division and its regular distributors.
850 Third Ave., New York N.Y. 10022

Trees

Reed pen, thinned ink on semi-absorbent paper, 5½ x 12 inches

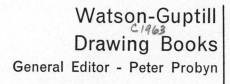

Watson-Guptill
C1963
Drawing Books
General Editor - Peter Probyn

TREES Colin Hayes

Contents

Introduction

Trees look quite obviously different from figures, houses, animals or chairs. Anybody who sits down to draw one may well feel that there is some special way of doing it, for trees (they differ from each other enough, let alone from anything else) are pretty daunting objects at first sight. What are the special secrets?

I have to start by saying that the secrets of drawing trees are, in the main, the secrets of drawing. Indeed, I must ask the reader to bear with me in curbing, for a page or so, his enthusiasm for trees; I am really trying to save him time in the long run.

It is not much good, for instance, telling people to begin drawing trees by reducing them to cubes, cylinders and cones (as is often suggested) if they cannot draw cubes, cylinders and cones with any assurance. But the ability to represent such simple objects in depth is the departure point for drawing anything, and this means we must try to understand clearly the functions and powers of at least some of the marks that can go to make up a drawing.

When Constable or Rembrandt made their magic-looking representations of trees in pencil or pen-and-wash, 'magic' is what many people regard as the whole process, as if the means by which these drawings were brought about were mysterious and inscrutable. And yet the magical element in master drawings lies in their superior intelligence, authority and sensibility, and it is this last which defies ultimate analysis. The actual means are usually perfectly clear if we go to the trouble of sorting them out.

Now this is no place for a History of Drawing. It is enough to say that Constable, looking at an actual elm, had more marks meaning more things at his disposal than had a medieval illuminator drawing a flat conventionalized apple tree of Eden. As most readers will feel that Constable's idea of a tree's appearance is more like their own than that of the 12th century, it is worthwhile to wonder about some of the marks which go to make possible what we think of as representational drawing. I would like the reader to follow me in gathering a few basic devices to stock his draughtsman's equipment.

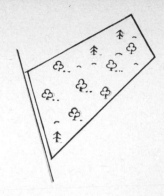

How to Start

The simplest form of drawing equipment is a line and its simplest form of use is the ideograph. Ideographs were used as a rudimentary form of writing, when all that was required was to convey a general idea. 'A line round an idea' that makes its point needs no elaboration. Look at a 1 inch to the mile Ordnance Map. You will find that it recognizes two kinds of trees, a kind of double-barbed arrow, or a clover-leaf.

The map does not mean that there is a tree looking like one of these shapes at such and such a point, or even that there is one tree. It merely tells you of the presence of trees, conifer-type and deciduous-type.

Nevertheless it is a sort of drawing, and worth mentioning because it shows in a rudimentary way how drawing is a language which has to be accepted and understood.

In order to represent an individual tree with some degree of realism, we must enlarge the vocabulary a little. With an inadequate vocabulary you will find yourself using a line to say what you know about trees instead of what you can see about them.

Some tribal societies do this intentionally, for symbolic purposes. They may know that a summer tree is covered with leaves (1), or that fish are covered with scales (2). But to them branches and backbones are more elemental properties of these objects. This is a perfectly reasonable attitude, but it is not quite what we need here.

However it does not to do despise symbols, because except by slavishly copying

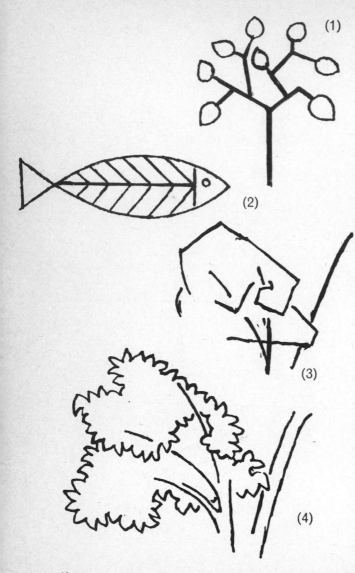

(1)

(2)

(3)

(4)

every leaf in Nature, we must always symbolize to some extent when we draw a tree.

Symbols begin clearly to talk the language we want when they start overlapping (3). A tree in an Indian miniature might look something like this (4). The parts are flat and formalized but there is an intimation that depth exists.

But lines can be made to mean more than this. If we put a line round the observed shape of an actual tree as accurately as we can, we shall find that we now have what is in effect a silhouette of an object, not a symbol for one. (Though look at master drawings of trees and see how they seem to retain the feeling for symbolism, however remotely.)

A silhouette line is the first active step towards realism; it shows what your intentions are.

I shall call a line a 'contour' only when it is consciously used to describe a surface or plane seen edgeways on. Contour lines can transform themselves into exposed surfaces.

At this stage I am going to summarize

these points, and add some more, by inventing a curious landscape.

Let us imagine that we are sitting with pencil and paper out of doors. In front of us are three objects, a box and a large beach ball both quite near us, and in the middle distance (so that it appears about the same size) a cone-shaped tree.

Diagram (5) shows the simplest thing we can do to describe the situation - which is to put an outline as accurately as possible round the outside of the objects and note where the horizon cuts them.

These are silhouettes. They do not tell us anything about depth or solidity.

We can help ourselves towards depth by moving our position until the objects overlap (6), as in our Indian miniature.

The objects are not yet solid, but there is the suggestion that one comes behind the other.

This suggestion is enhanced still more by allowing the front silhouette to break the line of the one behind it (7).

But how are the objects to be made solid with lines?

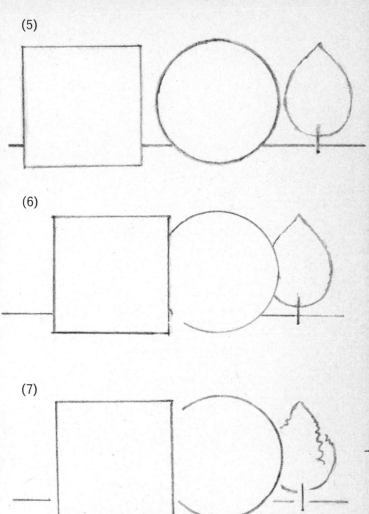

(5)

(6)

(7)

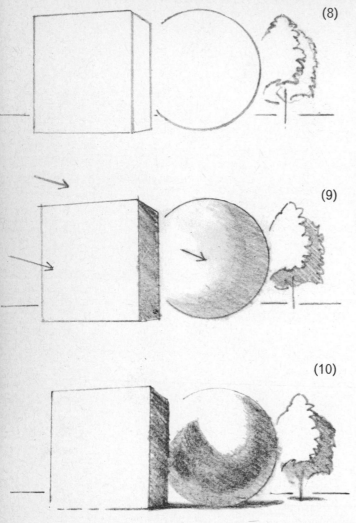

(8)

(9)

(10)

If we turn the box so that we can see another side (8) we can suggest that it has three dimensions; and we then see that the tree too has a front and a side. But we have done nothing to help the beach ball.

Now is the time to notice that the objects are illuminated (indeed they would be invisible if they were not). On the grayest of days solid objects disclose light and shade (9). With this we can give form to the beach ball and enhance that of the box and the tree.

We have now collected a number of devices - the silhouette, the overlap, the broken silhouette, and the shadow on one side of an object.

Now let us command a sunny day and we shall see that we have another sort of shadow, the *cast shadow* (10). This helps to explain the relative positions of cube and sphere and the fact that all the objects rise from the surface of the ground. You will see that some reflected light from the ground strikes back into the shadows. Before I can release you from this monotonous landscape I must introduce a storm cloud (11). Some of the outlines we have relied on so far are now suggested by the explanatory pattern of the shadows. It is important to notice that the background tone merges in places with the shadows on the objects.

Here are a few more 'devices'. It sometimes happens that 'sectional' lines, equators as it were, exist round objects like tree trunks, and these can be very useful in explaining their solidity (12). But they should be used with discretion; to invent them where they do not exist is a somewhat debased form of drawing.

A soft edge to a shape usually gives the feeling of a form gently curving out of view, where a sharp line corresponds to a sharp edge in nature.

Remember however that the insides of shadows soften everything - edges, lines and contrasts.

I have tried to summarize these points in this drawing. One final preliminary word about drawing in general - don't devote your efforts to making your drawings look clever. Skill comes with practice in trying to render the shapes of things.

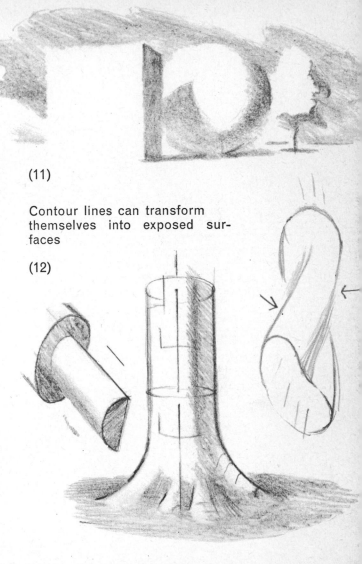

(11)

Contour lines can transform themselves into exposed surfaces

(12)

Simple Ideas of Structure and Growth

A knowledge of human anatomy can help the artist to draw the figure. A tree is a living functioning thing too, so that it is a good idea to know a little about its growth and working. But remember that many great artists have got on very well with a very limited scientific knowledge; some of them would say that it is possible to know too much about objects in a specialised way, so that you find yourself drawing with preconceived ideas instead of from observation.

A tree lives by attracting air and sunshine with its leaves. These combine with the substances drawn up from the ground through its roots, trunk and branches to provide food for further growth, and this act itself maintains the circulation of sap in summer. A tree is designed, therefore, to catch light and air through its leaves in the summer, and each leaf strives to present itself to the light. Because of this trees which appear from the outside to be solid with leaves are in fact comparatively hollow of leaves in their interiors. The trunk is, as it were, both a pillar and an artery, which diminishes in size and strength upwards, as its twin tasks lighten. Its roots serve both to draw in food and to provide an underground foundation for the tree. Trees grow bigger, as everyone knows; but their outer skins are not as elastic as ours. They crack, die, but remain as bark protecting the more delicate wood underneath.

This is all very elementary and well-known, and of course whole books far longer than this have been devoted to the scientific subject of tree growth and anatomy. That is the danger: let us stick to the simple things which will help us to begin, not hinder us.

We know, then, that trunks get thinner, and that leaves congregate usually towards the outside air and light. Are there any more 'visual' rules which can be relied on?

Trees vary so much from species to species, and from one example to another of the same species, indeed some are so prone to deformity, that I hesitate to use the word 'rule' about the following points in a strict sense.

This however is a 'working proposition' - the trunks of trees do not usually become thinner in an arbitrary way until they are finally dissipated into branches. The area of the cross-section of a trunk is reduced by the similar area of the branches which successively grow from it. As branches divide up they reduce themselves in the same way: this principle gives you a clue to estimating thickness of trunks and branches - particularly in winter trees.

Upward spiral growth is a common feature of plants, and not least of trees. It is more evident in some species than others. Among trees which commonly show a pronounced spiral twist (helical, properly speaking) are apples, pears, horse chestnuts and sycamores. As trunks tend to grow in this way, so do branches tend to spring from trunks rather in the way of the spokes on a spiral staircase.

Is there any sort of order to the intervals at which branches spring from trunks, and from each other? In some plant forms a natural proportion recurs time and again which the ancient Greeks called the 'Golden Section' and used in their architecture. It is a distance cut so that the smaller part is to the larger part as the larger part is to the whole: $BC : AB = AB : AC$.

You will find trees in many Renaissance paintings being made to obey this interval, for reasons of design. Do not expect to find trees in Nature dividing up according to this neat law; they are too individualistic. Nevertheless some kinds of trees display a visible tendency towards the 'Golden Section', notably conifers.

With the devices and information we have gathered, it is time to face the problem of developing an actual tree drawing from a simplest beginning, stage by stage.

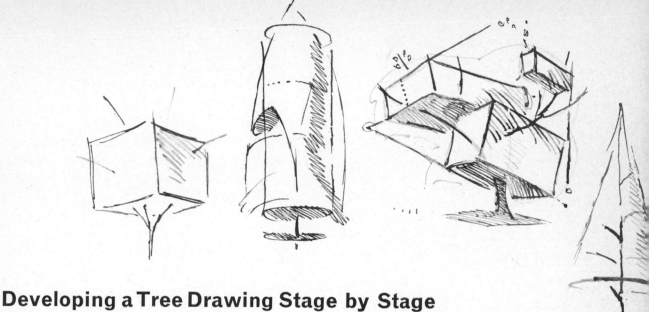

Developing a Tree Drawing Stage by Stage

How solid is a tree?

Most of the space occupied by a tree is clearly air. But it is best to begin by considering this space as a solid bulk with a top or point, sides, and underneath. This helps us to appreciate the tree form as a unit. We can knock holes and hollows into it later. Some trees are regular and compact, and so make this easy. Others send isolated branches and twigs out through the 'skin' of this solid.

How to begin a drawing depends on the subject, and what you want from it. There are no hard and fast rules, and while I have said 'consider this space as a solid', it is the mental process that matters. I do not mean that you should necessarily begin by constructing such a series of perspective boxes on the paper, but it will help you get into the habit of feeling their presence. The following pages set out a procedure of the sort that might be followed, in drawing an acacia.

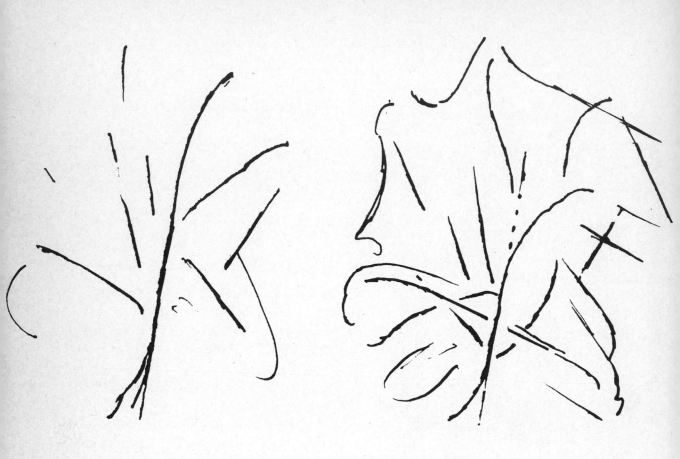

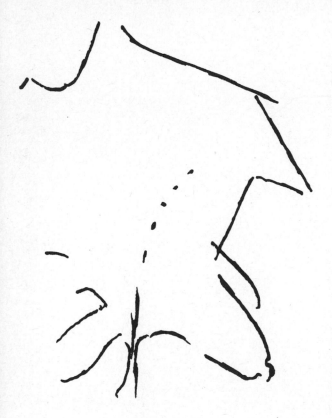

Action

A draughtsman must discover that solid objects possess the quality of 'action', even though they are not in movement. A tree's action is that of upward growth, while its branches search outwards, resisting the force of gravity. It is a safe rule to look first always for the 'action' lines. These 'lines' are simply a searching on the paper for the tree's living design.

You will find that the trunks and branches of most trees dart up and out in alternating straights and curves. Look for the straight lines of action. (A drawing all curves is usually weak, as the tree would be.) Then search for the 'silhouette' round the 'action' in very broad terms. You will find that it too curves and straightens, and presents you with a few simple directions.

We have been discovering the 'feel' of the tree as a flat pattern on the paper. Now we may begin to think of its solid bulk and here I have likened the tree to a sort of beehive. I have of course thickened

the relevant lines to show what I am talking about: they can be kept quite light in the actual drawing and will take their place without having to be rubbed out. If you look at the foliage and compare it with this simplified conception you will find that some of the lines of leaves suggest where there are in effect 'sectional lines' round the tree. The tree hints at what the parallels of latitude and meridians of longitude on a globe make plain: seize on these hints. Remember another thing about globes. If you can see one pole inside the silhouette, you can't see the other. This is likely to be true of the tops and underneath of trees. The more you develop this idea the more the action line of the trunk will begin to take its place as an 'axis' through the middle of the mass.

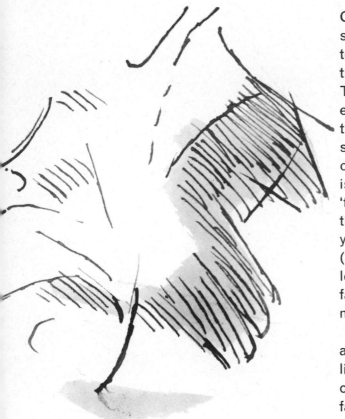

Light and Shade

One of the things about the light and shade on a tree that often puzzles people to begin with is the fact that the whole tree usually looks dark against the sky. There may seem at first to be little difference between one side of a tree and the other. Only the 'holes' and the underside are obviously dark. Nevertheless except in a very flat gray light the difference is there to be found. Try comparing the 'tones' (or degrees of light to dark) with the ground rather than the sky, which you must mentally reduce in tonal value (as painters have to). Tilt your head and look at the tree sideways on. The unfamiliar view will reveal things you have not noticed.

First of all find which side of the tree as a whole is the darker. If you have the light behind you, both sides will darken off as they turn away from the surface facing. You will notice this more clearly by looking at another tree in the distance, where the small scale simplifies these

points. The underside is in shadow.

If you have some watercolours try on another piece of paper to wash in the general masses of shadows to see what sort of a flat pattern they make. Best of all try this on some very thin paper so that you can trace your washes over your line drawing. (If you make a brush study like this, to use and throw away, it will probably be worth keeping.) Refer this pattern to your tree drawing and you will find that it represents the shadows on the under-side of the fronts of the leaves: your sectional lines will tell you how the main shadows 'go'. Some of the shadow pattern will be where you can see right through to the inner surface of the tree's opposite side, and this is usually darker. Now we can look at what happens to the trunk, and how it enters shadow as it thrusts up into the tree. The action lines of the drawing emerge here and there as branches.

Now that we have arrived at the main substance and structure and have given our drawing a sense of light, it is time to look once again at our tree's silhouette. Our original general silhouette is probably half obscured by now, but we must allow it to go on controlling the main shape, or the drawing will lose punch and character. However, we can see that the edge of the tree is made up of small 'actions' just as the whole tree is made up of large ones. Groups of leaves form a pattern of movement which continue across the drawing and form the edges of smaller overlapping shapes inside the drawing.

An important thing to notice is that once you have introduced the element of light you will rarely be able to put a line like a wire right round a shape. It will nearly always disappear into shadow or behind another line somewhere, and this is where the line breaks.

I have supplemented the drawing with a wash of tone, and put in the cast shadow of the tree to relate it to the ground. Simplify light and shade. The whitest

paper and the blackest indian ink will give you only a fraction of Nature's tonal range, and you must accept this fact. My advice is to choose four or five degrees of tone ('gray') from light to dark, and stick to them. The varied tones of Nature must be made to fall into one or other of your chosen categories.

Reed pen and wash on cartridge.
These simple tones unify the
drawing and give it bigness.
$6\frac{1}{2}$ x 5 inches

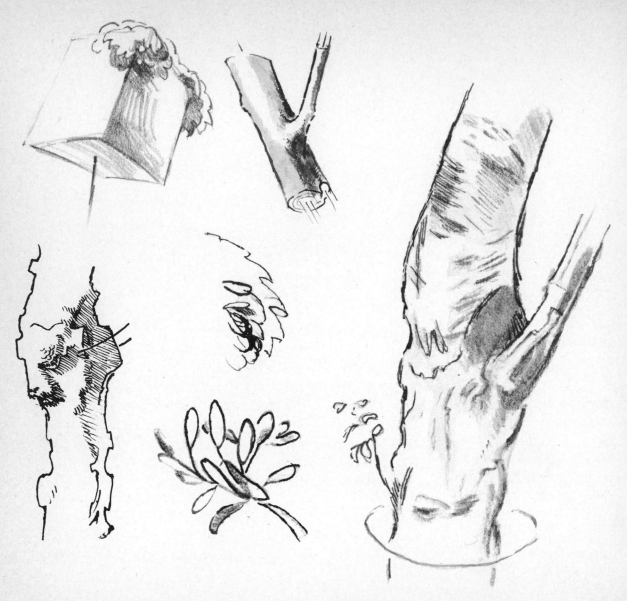

Using Detail

How far should you take a drawing?

It is a good idea, when teaching yourself by practice, to take a drawing a little further than you easily can, for in this way you learn. Maintain your interest as long as you can. But stop the moment you have lost it; otherwise you will only kill the drawing.

Drawings usually founder on misplaced detail. Nobody can tell you finally what to put in a drawing and what to leave out; but you may be sure that details are at their most valuable when they are contributing to an explanation of the main form. These, too, are the details which most forcibly suggest other similar ones. Look at a Rembrandt landscape drawing carefully and you will be surprised at the extent to which it is composed of acutely selected and carefully drawn detail. You may expect to find such details, for instance, at moments where larger forms join together - trunks and branches. Certain details seem to help express the decorative character of a particular tree very clearly, but be wary of decoration for its own sake.

A particularly important detail, and the most commonly neglected, is the shape of a gap or 'window' through a tree, or between one tree and another.

There is a fascination in drawing individual leaves and twigs, as we shall see. Sit almost under a tree and a single leaf may be a powerful element in your drawing. You are certainly likely to draw a tree

the better for knowing what shape its leaves are.

But there comes an optimum distance between you and the subject after which the single leaf is an act of self-deception; you cannot really see it, and you are either letting your observation slacken, or you are becoming a conscious symbolist.

Don't draw what you can't count - at least not if you are a realist. This is a piece of old advice, but I believe it marks the moment at which you must realize you are looking at groups of leaves, not single ones.

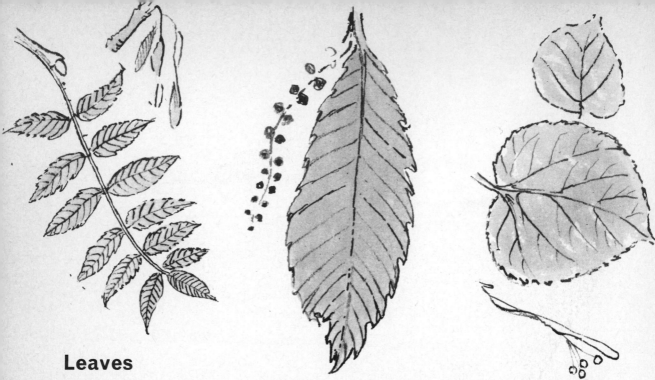

Leaves

It may be a mistake to draw leaves which you cannot count. Nevertheless the single leaf of a species sets the character of a group of those leaves, which in turn help to make up the character of the whole silhouette of the tree. This is why I introduce a few leaves, before I come on to the entire trees to which they belong.

An ash leaf is long and slender. Because it is really a series of leaflets making up one open leaf it is particularly decorative. There are usually about six pairs of leaflets, with an odd one at the end, to each whole leaf. They group into compact, heavy arabesque clusters. The twig is correspondingly strong to bear the weight.

A sweet chestnut leaf is a large individual, nine inches or so long with serrated teeth and catkin flowers hanging from its base in early summer. Its clumps of leaves, very compact and ornamental,.

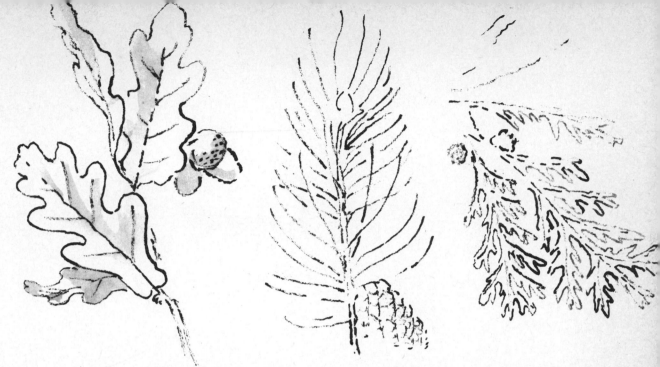

give this tree in full leaf an exceptionally pattern-like texture.

The lime, by contrast, has a round smooth heart-like leaf and delicate slender twigs. The leaves characteristically overlap and combine into larger, but lighter and more scattered, groups than on the sweet chestnut.

The common oak possesses the most familiar of leaves. They grow very thickly on the twig, often in tight, bunched groups, which are associated with the dark 'windows' between them.

Here is a quite different sort of leaf - the Scotch pine. It is a conifer whose leaves last over two years. Their long thin needles splay out round the cones and go together to give the tree's spiky Gothic silhouette.

And finally the cypress whose fronded leaves make their tight, drooping, column up the straight trunk.

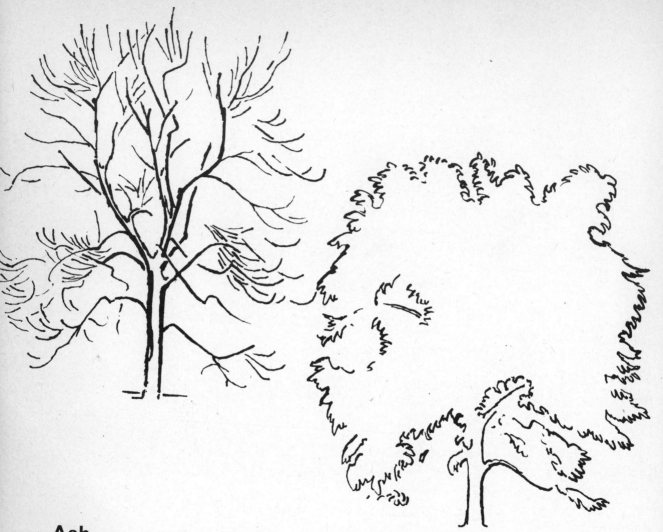

Ash

Silhouettes in Winter and Summer

This section I intend as a short 'Heraldry' of trees.

Learn to recognize, if you do not already, the way in which most trees signal their identity in summer and winter. Like heraldic devices on shields, which were, at least originally, meant to be recognizable from a distance, so trees are symbols of their own species. If you know what tree you are drawing you will not minimize its characteristics.

We have seen the leaves. Now let us look at five of these trees as a whole.

The Ash is both strong and graceful. Notice its straight bole and elegantly curving branches. The downward glide, ending in the consistently upward hook, is characteristic. Its twigs make a heavy network. Clothed in summer its leaf groups descend in small graceful canopies.

The winter Chestnut is not so gainly, its thick trunk often dispersing itself so abruptly near the summit that it seems out of proportion. Its branches grope out with elderly angularity like the oak; it is a somewhat formidable looking tree in winter. In summer its leaf groups combine in cumulus-like masses to transform its character.

The Lime by contrast is even more elegant and slender in appearance than the ash. But it can be very tall, and its trunk is often thicker than you may suppose at a glance. Typically, its lower branches fan out almost horizontally while its upper branches hold in towards the vertical axis of the trunk. In summer this structure is often indicated by great gaps in the foliage half-way up, giving a view of the inner vault below the roof.

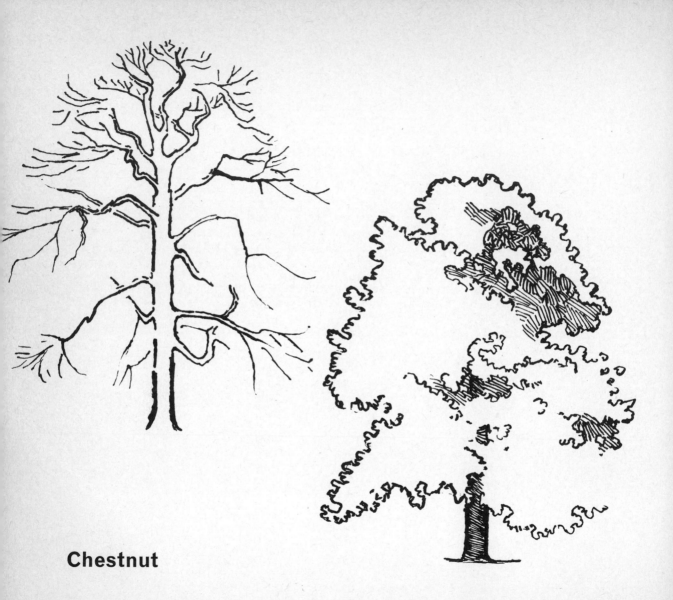

Chestnut

Lime

Oak

The Oak in winter is the most formidably naked of trees. From its short wide bole, it sends its enormously heavy branches (almost trunks in themselves) writhing out and up in a series of tortured but powerful gestures. The tightly bunched twigs with which these branches terminate carry closely packed bunches of leaves in summer.

Plane

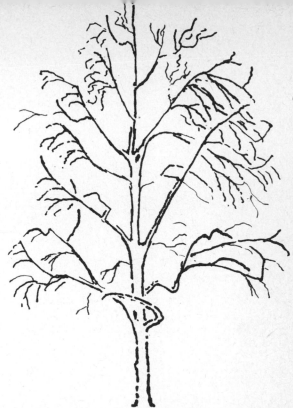

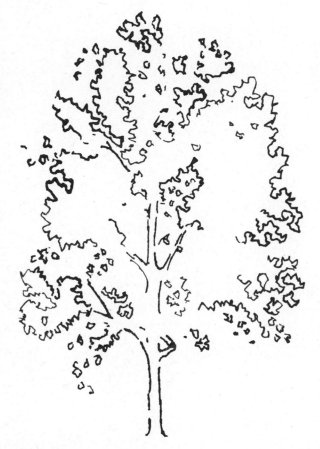

The resilient London Plane is among the happiest of urban decorations. While its scaling, flaky bark is its most familiar characteristic, its shape is also unmistakable. The straight, well proportioned bole separates into a kind of elegant disarray of slim branches and twigs. Its sparkling summer colour is an ideal foil to bricks and mortar.

Reed pen and thinned ink, 5½ x 8 inches

Trees in relation to each other

Few people want to learn how to draw trees so that they can produce endless isolated tree studies. Trees are gregarious and it is their varied association in the landscape that makes them really fascinating subject matter. Once we start looking at them from this point of view trees become at once more of a problem and more of an excitement.

What are some of the problems? Straight away there is a negative one. While we have necessarily been considering 'the tree' at close quarters, trees in the mass or in groups are, almost by definition, some distance away. Now distance makes things easier in some ways. The essential shapes present themselves much more readily, and we are spared a lot of confusing and demanding detail. But drawings which have merely avoided certain problems are likely to be boring - unless they have met others. In drawing woods and clumps of trees it is almost a problem in itself that we can get away with doing very little and apparently achieve some rather clever looking results. But they may not be worth much!

Yet there are plenty of things to be considered. First of all there is the matter of tonal recession. Out of doors, tonal contrasts rapidly diminish into the distance, although it is not always immediately apparent. Varieties of circumstances may make distant patches of shadow look black when really they are a pale gray. One safeguard against 'digging a hole in the distance' is to remember what I said earlier about making a simple tonal arrangement and sticking to it. When you have decided what tones you are going to use you have made a start, but you have still to sort out all the different degrees of light and shade in front of you. I was once, as a student, given some advice which I have always found helpful. Do not, as seems the obvious thing, try to decide the tonal value of a shadow by comparing it with a light tone. Instead, compare it with another and perhaps darker shadow. Compare, that is to say, darks with darks, half tones with half tones, and lights with lights. You will be able to sort out your tonal values more quickly and subtly, and you will not finish a wash drawing with the distressing discovery that a shadow in the left distance has got hopelessly out of gear with the right foreground.

Another problem with trees in mass is to find a coherent design. I have not embarked on this topic yet. Single trees which are carefully studied 'from the whole to the part' will go a long way to designing themselves: they are in their own way logical structures.

Groups of trees, woodlands and copses conform to some order, too, for they are dependent on the lie of the land; but the order is much more difficult to see. Yet it is still a matter of discovering the action. I have tried to show what I mean in some of these accompanying landscape drawings.

3B pencil and watercolour, 4½ x 10 inches

Pen and sepia, $4\frac{1}{2}$ x 9 inches

The nature of the terrain, its flatnesses, ridges, undulations and hollows will always set up an underlying rhythm to a wooded landscape; and, as I have already mentioned, distance helps us here. But it must help in a positive way. In the distance you will see compactly presented the sorts of rhythm and massing which are difficult to sort out in the foreground. Nature has a way of hinting at a kind of formal geometry and it is necessary not to impose contrived designs on it, but rather to impose the order which it possesses already. But Nature will seldom do your selecting for you: it is for you to decide where to place your horizon, where the limits of your subject are to reach in the picture.

I am inclined to think that the shortcut dogmatic rules of design which are so often offered to the student are more dangerous than valuable. You will have discovered the main secret of designing a picture when you have a pictorial point to make, and can stick to it.

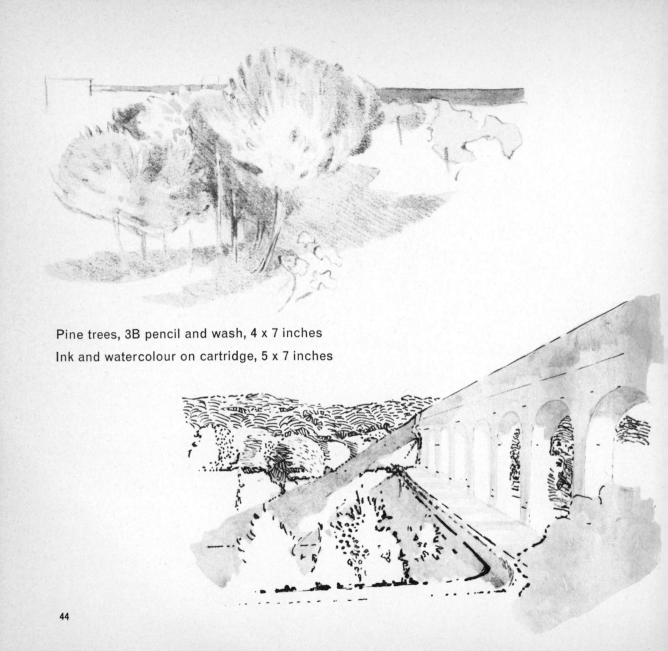

Pine trees, 3B pencil and wash, 4 x 7 inches

Ink and watercolour on cartridge, 5 x 7 inches

Horizon

V.P.

Centre

It will not have escaped notice that I have said nothing of Perspective methods as an aid to drawing. To this omission I must plead simple lack of space and refer the reader to the numerous text-books on the subject. Choose a simple one which deals with Perspective coherently, or you will find it becoming your master instead of your servant. Do not let it supplant the evidence of your eyes.

3B pencil on cartridge, 7 x 5½ inches

Reed pen and indian ink, $4\frac{1}{2}$ x $5\frac{1}{2}$ inches

Materials

It must be apparent to the most innocent beginner that no one man could have a need for all the items of drawing equipment offered to him in the catalogue of an artist's colourman. The reputable firms do not sell rubbish: everything is no doubt useful to somebody. But you can only acquire more than a small proportion of them if you want to equip yourself like the White Knight against every improbable hazard.

Unless you have money to burn it is better to discover what you need, than what you could have done without; my advice is to start modestly and add to your materials as practice demands rather than buying, for instance, large made-up kits of watercolours.

So I must make these suggestions on the understanding that it is only the individual artist who can finally decide which of the many possible materials and media suit him best.

First of all it seems sensible to think

about the surface on which you are going to work. Here I think simplicity is the best bet, at least to start with.

Those tinted and speckled papers which 'do half the work for you' are very seductive and can of course be used by the practised draughtsman in a positive way; but they very easily lead to slightness of statement and preciousness of effect which are just what the inexperienced should avoid. I have come to realize that my intentions in drawing are nearly always better served by a straightforward good quality white cartridge paper. This is true even when using wash and water-colour: the granulated effects to be derived from using very coarse grained rag papers are pretty, but except in the hands of the very skilful they become the perpetual happy accident. It is worth looking about to find a cartridge paper which is neither too shiny nor too soft; and of course the heavier it is the better it will carry full washes of colour. I prefer to carry separate sheets of paper, not all the same size, attached to a light board (hardboard, if thick enough, makes an excellent medium-sized drawing board) with large broad rubber bands. Rubber bands have the advantage that unlike clips and drawing pins they do not intrude into the rectangle on which you are working.

Notebooks are more convenient. If you buy the 'ring-back' kind, do not leave it too long before fixing your drawings with a fixative spray, as this otherwise efficient type of notebook rubs drawings very quickly.

The extra bother of a light camp stool is worth while; nothing is more irritating than not being able to sit where you want to. The light folding aluminium kind is just as good, and less heavy, than the traditional wood and leather tripod stool.

Knees and one's spare hand always seem to me enough, but if you must have a sketching easel (you need one of course for oil painting) buy one which is firm rather than elaborate.

Now as to the media of drawing. The pencil is the most familiar of tools; it is

unpopular with many people because they suppose some special facility to be necessary before it can produce a good drawing. But it is better to avoid this sort of facility anyway: nothing is handier or more flexible than a pencil if you are not daunted by it - but you must have a penknife to go with it. Buy a really good quality pencil, neither gritty nor greasy, and do not suppose that it is in some way more moral to draw with a hard pencil than a soft one. '6 H's' may be left in the hands of topographical surveyors; I find anything harder than a '2 B' somewhat intractable. A lot depends on the make and the quality of the paper you are drawing on.

Pen-and-ink. This can be difficult to use if you buy the tiny nibs for some reason associated with drawing. The best are the large, old-fashioned, pointed school nibs, without patent ball points or square cut ends. Watered down indian ink makes a flexible medium: though ink and water are liable to separate if not agitated·frequently. Quill pens are difficult

to cut but worth the effort, and produce a line which seems the most natural accompaniment to a wash. Other linear weapons are of course the various kinds of chalk and crayon, in pencil and stick form. These are particularly suitable for large drawings, and drawings in which much tone will be needed. Remember that most of these media, such as conté crayon and particularly charcoal, need fixing at once. One of the most attractive tools is the sharpened reed or stick (almost any hard wood) which dipped in ink can, with practice in cutting, be made to produce almost any kind of line you want; and this is a particular occasion when rough paper becomes a delight to use.

Pastel is a very difficult medium to use with more than slightness and charm: it is also one medium of which you do need a large supply of closely related colours. It is well to have a fair command of drawing before trying them or they will almost certainly disappoint.

Watercolour on the other hand can be

Pen, watercolour and coloured inks, 8 x 11 inches

a matter of very simple equipment. A few well chosen colours, one good medium sized brush and a palette (with of course a good supply of water) will stand you in better stead than an elaborate array of expensive equipment.

Watercolour is, in a sense, as difficult as you make it. Use it first as a tonal support for, and extension of, a linear drawing, and you will find the brush and colour possible to control - look at drawings by Poussin, Claude and Rembrandt.

Banana plantation. Brush, reed pen and ink, with wash, 4 x 8½ inches

Olive groves near Granada. Reed pen and ink, 4 x 8 inches

If you aspire to the elaborate technical tricks of cuisine which go to make the 'professional watercolour' so admired, then you are reading the wrong book. I believe the only 'technical tricks' which are any good are those which an artist invents for himself (and then not always!).

There are many varieties and combinations of materials which there is no space to mention, but whatever you choose you will do well to keep it as simple as possible; drawing is difficult enough without any additional worries. But do not starve yourself of your choice - take more paper than you intend to use; more water than you think you will need, an extra pencil or two. Finally, and most difficult of all, more time than you can spare.

Summing Up

A book which has no further pretensions than to introduce some of the basic problems of drawing trees must inevitably leave out far more than it contains. But drawing is a matter of 'first things first'; if I have named and illustrated only a few specific trees, I hope I have put the reader in the way of learning about many more for himself. It is true that I have mentioned neither the locust nor the monkey puzzler; but the principles of drawing these trees, so different from each other, are the same as those of drawing an oak (so different from either). It is important to stress that, though your attitude to drawing may remain consistent through the rendering of many varieties of tree, there is no reason why this consistency should not express the utmost contrast of character between each kind. Contrast of character is something that the artist can only acquire a feeling for by practice: he will

achieve this more quickly by the habitual practice of observing contrast. If you are drawing an elm and cannot see what makes it so peculiarly elm-like, turn your back on it for a few minutes and make a rapid drawing of some other tree if you can see one, a beech or a walnut. Turn back to your elm and you will have a few moments when its characteristic proportions, movements and groupings of foliage announce themselves with startling clarity. These are moments to seize on in drawing; get down what is fresh in your mind, and no matter if the results are a little crude or messy, they will have the force of conviction.

Remember that trees do not grow out of the air against blank white backdrops, though it is often made to seem so in drawings of them. It is not necessarily enough to scribble 'study' at the bottom of your paper and suppose that this absolves you from looking beyond the silhouette of your ash or your cedar. If you expect your tree to look 'alive' you are more likely to succeed if you give it somewhere to live, and few drawings are harmed by at least some indication of the ground - and background - of the subject.

I have written with a view to helping those readers whose interest in drawing is in the broad sense representational, and the suggestions I have made are directed towards the graphic explaining of actual visual experience. I would like to end by saying that of course this is only one aspect of drawing, and a comparatively recent one at that, where 'Nature' is concerned. Some maintain it has already had its day and to those whose object is flat decoration most of what I have said may seem irrevelant. But it may be that the artist who aspires to embellish wallpapers and fabrics with leaf and tree motifs will find the drawing of these curious things before nature a necessary basis of design. He may envy Renaissance Europe and the old Orientals their grand inherited traditions, but their pattern-books, alas, have been thumbed out of existence long since.

If we expect any more Art from a tree, we must go and look at it.